I Will Live Today!

ALABAMA CHRISTIAN
SCHOOL OF RELIGION
LIBRARY

Judith Garrett Garrison, M.Ed., L.S.W.
Scott Sheperd, Ph.D.

CompCare®Publishers

2415 Annapolis Lane
Minneapolis, Minnesota 55441

726.5
.55
1990

6201

LIBRARY OF CONGRESS
5
SEP 14 1990
COPY
CIP

© 1990 by Scott Sheperd and Judith Garrison
All rights reserved.
Published in the United States
by CompCare Publishers.

Reproduction in whole or part, in any form, including storage
in memory device systems, is forbidden without written
permission except that portions may be used in broadcast or
printed commentary or review when attributed fully to author
and publication by names.

Sheperd, Scott. 1945–
    I will live today / Scott Sheperd and Judith Garrison.
       p.   cm.
    ISBN 0-89636-223-0
    1. Critically ill—Psychology. 2. Adjustment (Psychology)
I. Garrison, Judith Garrett. II. Title.
R726.5.S5   1990   90-41463
155.9'37—dc20   CIP

Cover and interior design by Lillian Svec
Illustrations by Toshi Maeda

Inquiries, orders, and catalog requests should be addressed to
CompCare Publishers
2415 Annapolis Lane
Minneapoli, Minnesota 55441
Call toll free 800/328-3330
(Minnesota residents 612/559-4800)

6   5   4   3   2   1
95   94   93   92   91   90

"You shall be free indeed
when your days are not
without a care nor your nights
without a want and a grief,
but rather when these things
girdle your life and
yet you rise above them
naked and unbound."

—Kahlil Gibran

Peace &
Strength

PEACE

Purifying your spirit with knowledge
    of your goodness,
Easing your fear, anger, guilt, and
    other negative thoughts from
    your awareness,
Allowing the strength and energy of
    life to flow into your being,
Caring, healing prayers lift
    your tired body with them,
Elevating your spirit above the
    mundane and bathing you in
    the golden world of peace.

I am part of the universal
   consciousness.
I will open myself to the
   wisdom and strength that
   resides in the universe.

I don't need to search for peace.
   It is within me.

*P*eace guides me.

It leads me where I need
    to travel.
It stimulates my being to
    fulfill my destiny.

❦

I walked through the woods
today and found my spirit.

*L*isten carefully to the whispers
from within your being.
The fleeting images, the lingering
thoughts are keys to your inner self,
your deepest feelings.

Listen carefully to the whispers.
Allow yourself to know your
feelings, so you can resolve the
fearful ones and take comfort in
your hopes and dreams.

I am buried beneath the weight
    of my life.
I am crushed by the problems
    I experience.

And yet, there are times I sense,
if only for a moment, there
is something in me, in the deepest
core of who I am, that can free me
from this weight.

I refuse to accept the philosophy that
if only I have a "positive enough"
attitude I will be able to defeat
this disease.

That must mean everybody who died
just wasn't positive enough—
that they failed.

Who needs that pressure?

*L*et the image of death ignite
  in me the blaze of living.
Let me consume life as hungrily
  as a flame.
Let me be actively, passionately
  aware of each precious moment.

*W*hen I trust in myself,
    I am at peace.
When I feel the presence
    of love in my soul,
I am in touch with God
    and I have a sense of
    life that far transcends
    what I am aware of now.

I love.
I live.

I will gather strength
    from peace.

Saturate yourself with positives.
Read, or listen to, or view
    what is beautiful.
Let it surround you
    and encompass you.

Settle your being.
Get it clear in your mind
    what it is you want.
Remember you have the inner
    power to obtain it.

*T*he leaves are dancing
merrily in the light
of summer's sun.
They are part of the
present moment.

I pray, not as a beggar
asking for favors,
But as a riverbed opening
itself to the life-giving
waters of its source.

AMRIDGE UNIVERSITY
LIBRARY

Southern Christian University Library
1200 Taylor Rd.
Montgomery, AL. 36117

*A*t times I feel the winds of illness
have made a barren landscape of
my life.
I can no longer see mountains to be
climbed in the distance.

But then I look around me and
I realize that I am soaring
above the mountains.
They look so small from my new
perspective.

*W*hen I hurt in the present, at
  least I have something I can
  contend with.
When I fear the future, I make
  myself helpless.
The future is beyond my control.
  The present is not.

I am worthwhile.
I have dignity.
The beauty of God is in me.

I can feel the love of my
Higher Power strengthening me!

*T*here are days when the details—
the endless day-to-day details—
almost block out the beauty and
wisdom and pure joy of simplicity.

Now, though my life sometimes feels
bombarded by doctors and
tests and medicines,
I have learned to remember the
simple beauty of a smile,
a sudden laugh, a touch.

May the strength of that simplicity
stay with me and help me reach a
deeper peace.

Shadows of the past are vague
and the future is too distant
    to come into focus.
Now is brightly illuminated
    and richly colored.

Today I will remember to keep
    my mind in the present.
Now is all I have.
Now is all anyone has.

*O*pen
yourself gently
like a rose
to the sunshine
of love.

Let
the quietness
within you
explode into the
beauty of inner light
and awareness.

*W*e don't always appreciate
the fullness of life.
The trunk of a tree is alive,
but its gnarled structure seems
to be still and hard and cold.
Yet if we touch it, it touches
us back.

I must be willing to accept joy
before it will ever replace misery.

Although I have sickness in me,
  I also have wellness in me.

I will focus on the wellness,
  and allow it to overcome
  the sickness.

When I think about my youth,
now past, I remember myself . . .
     . . . as a strong seeker of life;
     . . . as one who accomplished tasks
        with strength and effortlessness;
     . . . as a contemplative philosopher.

Some things have been changed
    by time,
but my spirit is still as strong
    as ever.

I will trust my sense of myself.
When I am tired, I will rest.
When I am energized, I will act.
But through all this, I will *be.*

Starlight mystifies us;
    it gives us hope.
It causes us to be filled
    with awe at the vastness
    of the heavens, and our
    smallness, as well as
    our importance.

*I*t would be nice if this
wasn't happening
        but it is.

It would be nice if there
weren't any pain or suffering
in the world
        but there is.

It would be nice if I could
handle this
        and I can.

*E*very day can't be a good day.
But within each day—those
long twenty-four hours—there
are a few minutes or even
seconds when something good
or special happens.

Those moments are as powerful
as the frail flame of a candle
that can light an entire dark room.

*T*he earth turns
slowly,
steadily,
predictably,
peacefully,
in the vastness of space.

It glows with a beautiful light,
the light of life.

When I look for peace
   and find turmoil,
When I look for wisdom
   and find ignorance,
When I look for courage
   and find terror,
Most likely, I have found
   what I was looking for.

For how would I recognize peace
      if there wasn't turmoil?
And doesn't wisdom grow
      from ignorance?
And courage only matters when
      I am face to face with terror.

*M*essages come from God in
delicate ways . . .
>   . . . the softness of twilight
>   . . . the crescent moon
>   . . . the morning star
>   . . . the color of a rose.

If we are too busy,
too distracted,
we might miss them altogether.

*B*EAUTY

Being, oneness, captured in the
    physical world,
Eluding time, definition, limits,
    it dwells in a space all its own.
Always seeking awareness of its
    presence—a glimpse of a
    wildflower just off the path,
Uplifting the burdened spirit, it
    pulls the soul above itself,
    opening to all who are willing
    to see,
Tempting us to the infinite, the
    place where beauty lies.
You may succumb to its temptation,
    accept its precious gift.

May the beauty of life fill me with joy.

*L*ife is like a rainbow.

You can only appreciate the richness
of its beauty when you experience
both the sunshine and the rain.

*T*he wind is blowing across the
    meadow, through the woods.
The trees are weaving and the
    animals scurrying to hide.
The clouds are thick and moving
    fast. A storm is coming.

I won't try to run, because I
    know the storm is not an enemy.
It will not swallow me up.
It will pass.

And I will survive with strength,
                 dignity,
                 courage,
                 and love.

Simplicity has a way of
　　calming the aching spirit;
　　lessening the complexities of life;
　　easing the pressures; and
　　freeing my spirit.

Thanks for today.
I will do the best I can.

Thoughts crowd our minds,
swirling like snow in a storm.

Let your thoughts be quieted,
and fall gently to the ground
like snowflakes, softly drifting
down to beautify the landscape
of your mind.

*E*very being that lives, grows.
Each will grow despite harsh
conditions and beautify its
surroundings.

Like a tundra bloom,
the most striking and beautiful
flower is the one that blossoms
despite frigid, brutal conditions.

Sometimes when you take a hammer
and smash a dust-brown, craggy rock,
inside you find the purest colors,
glittering from tiny smooth surfaces,
like the sparkling facets of a jewel.
It is here you find the rock's spirit.

Today I will remember the ancient
wisdom: "Purity of spirit brings
an end to all sorrow."

I know there is a power in me
that brings peace and love
    and serenity.

Some call it God.
Some call it a universal life force.

The word doesn't matter—
    the peace, love, and serenity do.

*T*he games of the past are gone.
My ego has been peeled,
layer after layer,
until all that
exists is
my core.

And it is beautiful!

*F*rom the wellspring of my life,
   resurging, overflowing,
   full of gentle motion,
   energy that renews me rises up
   from deep within.

Volumes of words can't grasp
   the indefinable essence of the
   spirit that fills my body now,
   and until it is time to depart.

I want to name the essence, so
   I will call it peace.
Today I will remember that
   I am filled with peace.

Hope &
Courage

*P*eace.
The smooth hum of being.
Pure stillness, yet pure energy
guides all of my actions.

Hope.
A beacon assuring me that
peace is there for me.
My energy remains focused on hope,
aware that illness cannot overcome
my spirit.

Love.
The source of all energy.

I need to sit somewhere
and clear my mind.

I cannot fight worry;
    it feeds on the struggle.
But I can let go of it.

In letting go of worry,
    I will find peace.
In finding peace, I will
    feel hope again.

*I*f I hold in my fear, anger,
    tears, and anxiety,
Confusion overwhelms me in the
    jumble of medical details.
Isolation prevails as I draw deeper
    within myself—trying to
    understand, trying to protect
    my fragile being.

Feeling backed to the edge
    of my abilities,
I turn and am overwhelmed to
    feel the depth and presence
    of God, feeding me new
    strength and comforting me.

I can move forward again!

*M*y spirit moves my body.
My spirit is healthy.
My spirit is alive.

*W*hen I allow myself to open
onto a quiet sea of peacefulness,
my inner fears and confusion
can subside.

The churning waves of doubt
and distraction die down,
like the ocean flattening out
for a time.

At least for now, I will float
on this peaceful surface.
At least for awhile,
I will let myself relax
and feel free.

*S*avor this moment.
Don't let it drift away
like leaves floating on a stream.
Notice it, watch it, live it.

I learn something every day,
    except when I spend my time
    wishing today were different.
Then I just mark time.

Sometimes I cry
    at the littlest thing.
Sometimes I laugh
    at the littlest thing.
Maybe that's good.

Maybe before I never even saw
    the littlest thing.

If I "lose it" once in awhile,
    so be it.
Who says I've always got to keep
    it together?
I never claimed to be a saint.

*L*ife doesn't always happen
    as we would like.
It takes twists and turns
    that catch us off guard.

We must keep our spirit buoyant
    and free to enable ourselves
    to flow with the challenges
    life presents.

*I*llness is a fog that shrouds
    our spirit.
It limits our vision and our
    perception and disorients us.
Inner healing breaks through the
    fog, like shafts of sunlight,
Illuminating our awareness and
    restoring inner strength.

*H*opes and dreams
do not reside
in the future.
They are now.
They reflect our ability
to see the wonders of life.

I can still hope and dream even
if my future appears uncertain.
My mistake was thinking that
it ever was assured.
In fact, now I can use this
uncertainty as an incentive
to live each day the best I can.

Sometimes I feel so lost and
lonely, it seems like my mind
and heart are trapped in a fog.

But when I quit struggling,
the sunshine of my spirit
clears the clouds,
lifts the fog, and
helps me find my way.

*K*eep your dreams close to you.
Cradle them as you would
     your child.
They are precious.

*T*ake a journey inside
a nautilus shell,
slowly turning inward
on an intricate, shining
pathway until you reach
a secure, protected center.

I am drifting in a vast ocean
   of illness.
I look around me and my isolation
   seems too much to overcome.
Then your caring breaks through
   my bleak illusion with the
   suddenness of the sun breaking
   through in the midst of dark
   clouds of storm.
I feel the warmth of your presence.

Love is not measured by actions.
Love is an energy that sustains
the giver and the receiver
just by existing.

*I*t is said that all life comes
     from the sea.
We equate life with the sea.
When we are alive, we are immersed
     in the sea of life.
We float and drift and dive in
     the waves of living.

❧

*D*rift softly into the night.
Let your being glide on the
gentle breath of pleasant dreams.

*T*he challenge is never
   in facing death.

The challenge is always
   in facing life.

I will not fight against death
    because that is a fight someday
    I will lose, and I do not want
    to leave life on a losing note.
Instead, I will fight for life and
    all its joy and beauty.

Then, when the day comes that I must
    go, I will leave behind a gift.
    My spirit.

My spirit will carry a message,
    saying that love, beauty, hope,
    and courage can be found in
    the darkest times.

*F*ear will kill the spirit
long before any disease
will kill the body.

But fear can't exist without
my permission.

*W*ords from the Bible are
often comforting, no matter
what your religion:

"Let not your hearts be
troubled, neither let them
be afraid."
                    —John 14:27

At times I become frightened
when I think of death.

There are so many unknowns . . .
       . . . so many questions,
       . . . loved ones to leave behind,
       . . . unfinished business,
       . . . unfulfilled dreams.

But then I realize that
I am still alive!
And every moment is a new chance.

*T*his disease is not *my* disease.
This problem is not *my* problem.
Who would want to own such a thing?
It is *a* disease in *my* body.
It is *a* problem in *my* life.

I don't need to make this worse
    by fighting for ownership.

*T*he ways of the past seem meaningless.

Now I am focused on the
   pulse of living.
Now I am concentrating only on
   the things that matter.

I am amazed that it is so simple,
   living and loving one day at a time.

I am not alone.

There is a power that
holds me, comforts me,
and most of all,
loves me.

 S ecurity is not in a lab report.
Security is not in a CAT scan.
Security is in my spirit
and my heart.

It is in me.
It is me.

*T*o die physically is no disgrace—
   it happens to the best of us.
To die spiritually is no disgrace—
   but it is surely unnecessary.

*D*eath is part of life.

I will accept death when it comes,
but I can still fight to stay alive.

*T*he future is only a thought.
The past is only a thought.
The present can become lost
  in these thoughts
  or enriched by them.

I choose enrichment.

*I*llness strikes and we are tossed
and tumbled into heavy surf.
Torments of pain and fear take
control of our bodies.
Finally, we lie exhausted,
beached on the sand.
Perhaps the sea barely
laps at our feet.
Perhaps the ghost crabs of death
whisper in our ears.

We must gently push ourselves
to wade back into the sea of life.
We must overcome the surf,
dive through the breakers
of illness that try again
to smash us onto the beach.
We must immerse ourselves once
more in the tides and flow of living.

I accept the fact that I am
      afraid at times.

Fear is not an enemy, but rather
      a friend whom I greet with
      graciousness, only to find
      that it must leave quickly,
      because the brightness of my
      other friend, Love, is more
      than fear can handle.

*B*ecoming aware of the possibility
of death has its good points.

It makes me aware of limits.
It makes me know I must get on
with my life now.

I can't arrange the future
   to meet my own needs.
I am part of a greater whole
   and, knowing that,
I seek to find strength in
   the feeling of acceptance
   and belonging.

I have learned something
from the situation I'm in,
or, perhaps more accurately,
I've been reminded of something—
I want to live with passion!

I want to embrace life every
moment and feel its power
surging into my soul.

No matter what my physical body
is doing or how it feels,
I will celebrate the miracle
of another day.

*T*here are no answers
to the questions I have.

But, if I allow myself
to let these questions go,
with the simple faith of a
child who cannot understand,
then I can turn easily
to the reality of *now*.

*T*here are times when I'm almost
overwhelmed by loneliness.
Even when I'm with the people
who care about me, I often feel
alone and isolated.

At those moments, maybe what I'm
feeling isn't loneliness, but
aloneness—awareness that even
those who love me most cannot
enter my experience totally.

At those moments of awareness,
I am open to the more subtle
recognition of a force or Power
or entity that joins me in my
aloneness and seems to be saying:
"Allow your aloneness
to become at-oneness."

*O*ften our situation is so clouded
that we can't see beyond them
to the universe of glowing stars
        the clouds obscure.

Even though they're hidden now,
the stars are still there.
The same is true of the many
        possibilities for me.

I will live today to the fullest
    I can.

If every day is lived that way,
I will have done what I can do.

*T*here is a new awareness in me.
I have been given, by this illness,
    an opportunity I hadn't expected.
Now I know how to experience
    the magic of being alive!

Love &
Wellness

*L*ove is energy,
energy unseen,
but powerful.

Love is strength.
Love is healing.

I will love.
I will be strong.
And I will heal.

Serenity is mine!

Wellness

Wash the illness from your body;
    gently, yet forcefully let
    it flow away from you.
Energy grows from deep within your
    spirit, totally filling you
    with a clean, golden warmth.
Love the energy. It radiates to
    all parts of your body and mind.
Love yourself, love others,
    love the infinite, love God.
Natural state of being, that good
    peace which is meant to be,
Eases your feelings and your soul
    into a calm, smooth place,
Sustaining your life, your loves,
    your hopes, and dreams,
Sustaining your Self, body and soul.
    You are so cared for and so loved.

*L*oneliness
is a barrier built by fear.

Aloneness
is different; it is one
of the conditions of life.
But one of the most positive
possibilities of life is
building bridges between
each other, so we can meet
and be together, separate,
but side by side.

At-oneness
is the meeting place where
there is the realization
and acceptance of love.

I will open myself to the care
of others.
I accept my need and appreciate
their caring.

*T*he closeness of others,
their warmth and caring,
comforts even my deepest pain.

Playfulness is the skittering of
    monkeys across the treetops.
It's the singing of birds for
    the pure pleasure of song.
It's the music of raindrops,
    bouncing on a canvas tent.
It's the joy of being alive.

As long as I live, I will look
    for the joy!

*T*he journey through illness
may be long and hard,
but it is made easier
by the company of friends.

You are with me.
I feel better!

I am still the curious child
who chased after fireflies and
marveled at their mysterious glow.

That glow is alive in me,
but I need to nurture it
and treasure it,
so it will guide me through
the dark moments of my life.

T here is nothing to be gained
    by anticipating misery.
I will find the peace I search for
    if I look within me.

Ultimately the choice is simple:
    I can quit, or
    I can move forward.

*M*ortality has got my attention,
I must admit it.
But where I put that attention
is up to me.

When my mind begins racing
with "what if's"
I can slow it down
with "and yet's"—
and yet I still have today.

Caring is within my capabilities.

I don't have to reach some
    predetermined level of
    performance.
I don't need to possess superhuman
    strength or endurance.
I am free to rest and refuel.

I give myself permission to take
    care of myself just as I would
    take care of anyone else I love.

*T*he fear fades when I sense the
strength of God in my soul.

Whenever I can overcome fear,
I am free to feel alive.

I love to watch how birds
    soar on the wind.
There appears to be such
    little effort, yet such joy.

I want to become like a bird
    and let my spirit soar
on the winds that are blowing
    through my life.

I will not be crushed against
    the rocks!
I will sense the rhythm, the
    flow, and react accordingly.
I will trust my inner guide.

When fear begins to invade my soul
and confusion muddies up my mind,
I reflect back to my childhood
and other fears and doubts I had.

Somehow I made it through
whatever challenge faced me,
not always with what I wanted,
but I did make it through.

And every time, I was
a little stronger after
than I was before.

*L*oving you
      has been
      is now
      will be
   a joy.

*W*e are tied to one another.
Our bond strengthens each of us
as we endure the storm of illness.

*D*o not fear being alone.

The peace of God will be
   with you.
The loving thoughts of friends
   will cover you.

*Y*ou can see past the exterior
    shell of my illness.
You and my own inner voice
    remind me that this
    illness is not the real me.

You have an inner strength
    that emanates from your being.
I feel it flowing from you to me
    and I know we can get
    through this.

Nobody gets out of here alive.
No doubt about it.
That doesn't mean I have to
    leave early, however.

I will not wait to be cured.
I will participate in the process
    of wellness.

*Y*our presence is like soft
 morning light,
illuminating the darkness
 of my loneliness.

You breeze into my awareness
 and splash the dull walls
of my illness with the vibrant
 colors of your friendship.

Sometimes it is difficult to
    accept help. I feel like
    a burden.
But I must trust in the process
    of love and life.

I am learning and growing as
    I accept help, because it
    is time for me to learn
    about acceptance.
Others are learning and growing
    from giving, because it is
    time for them to give.

In essence, I am giving while
    I am receiving.

"*I* like you."
"I love you."
Words have power.

I awake in the night
and I am fearful.
I think of you and
I am calm.

The presence of a friend
banishes the darkness of fear.

*I*t's astounding how much one little touch can accomplish.

Eyes touching eyes.
Skin touching skin.
Smile touching smile.
Heart touching heart.

I drift, asleep,
    overcome by the
    unpredictable force
    of my illness.

You awaken me and
    remind me I am still
    capable of loving.

You reach out to me,
    offering the gift
    of yourself—
    and I accept!

I need to let people know
    when I am lonely.
I cannot afford to play
    the games of:

> "If they were really my
>   friends, they'd know."
> "I'd just be in the way."
> "I'm becoming a burden."
> "I should be handling this better."
> "People don't want to hear
>   my problems."

Today I will remember to
    ask for what I need.

S ilence exists in me.
There are no words for the
    loss I feel.
The only sound I hear is
    the song of your caring.

T he bond we share is a warm
    fabric of protection from
    the outside elements.
Our friendship is a source
    of energy to me.

When I feel cold and alone,
    I reach for the comfort
    of your love.

Spend time . . .

> . . . thinking,
> . . . creating,
> . . . loving,
> . . . praying.

When my soul begins to tire,
the eyes of a child revive me.

We may not always receive answers.
Some things we just can't
    understand.
Maybe we aren't meant to.

We must trust that these unknowns
    are part of our pathway to growth.

The harder I try to get inner peace,
    the more frustrated I become.

Maybe there's a lesson there.

Save me from "friends" who make
me their project.
I am not a watch that needs to
be fixed.
I am a person who needs to be loved.

A hand given in love
brings with it
the power of healing.

*I*f you're coming to see me,
bring a smile once in awhile—
a real one—not one of those
tacked on jobs.

I want to feel the warmth
and hear a laugh.

*Y*our love shelters me
from the storm of my illness.

Your closeness comforts me.
Your willingness to help
seems inexhaustible.

Our relationship has been
challenged by my struggle for
survival, and we are strong!

*T*he peace of God is in me.
The strength of God surrounds me.

From the peace of my soul
will come the power of healing.

*W*hen the body is out of harmony,
   it becomes ill.
I will focus on putting my body
   back in harmony.

Today I will say, and say again
and again:

   "I am health."
   "I am wellness."

*T*his moment is precious.
I will not waste it.

I will LIVE for as long
    as I am alive.

ALABAMA CHRISTIAN
SCHOOL OF RELIGION
LIBRARY

Southern Christian University Library
1200 Taylor Rd.
Montgomery, AL. 36117